Pleasure Principles for Dri

Reclaiming

N

Lily Shepard

Pleasure Principles for Driven Women: Reclaiming Pleasure through Movement

Splendor House Publishing

Printed in the United States of America

ISBN: 979-8-9860039-0-0

ISBN: 979-8-9860039-1-7

Special discounts are available on bulk quantity purchases by book clubs, associations and special interest groups.

For information log on to *Lilyshepardmoves.com*

Cover Photo Credit: Talisa Lynn Photography

Contents

Dedication

This book is dedicated to the woman who desires a full and vibrant life.

The woman who is ready to move from self-loathing to self-acceptance

Who is ready to build an unshakeable belief in her intrinsic worth

Who is tired of hiding vulnerability behind independence

Who is eager to release the need to incessantly prove her worthiness

Who is willing to finally pay attention to her desires

Who is exhausted from dwelling in the masculine energy she feels is necessary to get ahead

Who knows that she can no longer afford to not prioritize her healing

The woman who is tired of looking at herself in the mirror and not recognizing the woman staring back at her

Who longs to express her sexuality without fear of judgment

Who wants to know herself better and trust herself more

The woman who has spent years in a toxic relationship with her body and is ready to build a healthy one

The woman who is afraid to be soft for fear she'll get walked over

Who feels the nagging pinch of resentment from years of being the one who does it all

The woman who has been cheated on, humiliated and discarded

Who amplifies her material success to distract from the fact that she's unfulfilled

Who thinks she needs drinks and dark lighting to be sexy

The woman who needs to know that achieving in a capitalistic society doesn't mean that you have to leave parts of yourself behind

The woman who no longer wants to feel guilty for wanting to feel good

Acknowledgements

To my family, thank you for loving on me and always being in my corner. To Jenn Wooten, thank you for being such an incredible teacher/mentor and encouraging me to expand my view of movement as a tool for healing. To Qi Dada, the seeds of MovFi were planted as a result of our work together. Thank you for bringing out the best in me as a creative collaborator. Raina Gradford and Melanie Holst-Collins. You two saw me through every step of this process. You were my sounding board and support system from the time this book was just an idea. Thank you for your confidence in me. To Leslie Youngblood, thank you for believing in me and being a continued source of inspiration. I've learned so much from you as an author and treasure our bond as family. To Melissa Miller, you put your trust in me in the very beginning and I love you for that. Thank you for seeing the mentor and healer in me before I had the confidence to boldly share those gifts. To Diana Haggerty, you generously opened your space to me during the pandemic and had it not been for me having a place to dance and express myself this book wouldn't be a reality. It was in that studio, on the dance floor that I decided that this book needed to be birthed. To Raoul Hernandez, you encouraged me to tell my story and share my love of dance with the world. Your support of me gave me the confidence I needed to do it.

Thank you.

Introduction

I was alone on stage with red lights illuminating my body and hundreds of eyes on me. I slowly walked around the pole, like a regal huntress selecting my prey so I could begin the process of emptying his pockets while his ego swelled from the attention he was getting. I went through the motions, moving in ways intended to look sexy to the audience but felt robotic and calculated to me. As I took to the stage at the world's biggest strip club in Las Vegas, it hit me: I had absolutely no connection to how my body was moving.

Here I was doing the most sexy, sensual job you could think of—making stacks of money most nights—and I didn't realize how disconnected from my body I really was. My mind was calculating how much more money I needed to make before I could leave, how much sleep I would get before it was time to take my daughter to school, what snacks I could eat that wouldn't make me feel bloated. Not only was my mind not present, but my body seemed to be angry at me. I remember being onstage and wanting to move differently but being afraid that veering from the formula would mess up my money. In that period of my life, my body only did three things: stripper moves, workouts, and rest.

I had forgotten how to move in ways that made *me f*eel good. On the surface, I had all of the things: a husband, a beautiful child, a home, and a steady source of income. But there was little fulfillment or creativity. I remember dancing on stage that night, swaying my hips as dollar bills rained down on me and thinking, *There has to be more.* Just as I was coming to this realization, the rug was pulled from under me. Literally two days after this moment of truth onstage at the club, I suffered public humiliation in my marriage when I found out my husband had been having an affair for quite some time, and I was the last to know.

As it unraveled, I became aware of multiple lies and deception that had taken place over the course of our five-year marriage. This resulted in divorce and threw me into single motherhood. It's interesting how we tend to fill in the blanks about who a person is based on who we wish them to be. Early on in my relationship to my ex-husband, I was confronted with several red flags that I chose to ignore because I had already drawn my conclusions. I recognized certain behaviors as red flags at the time, but I simply didn't trust my inner knowing enough to move on what I felt.

I was emotionally distraught, financially unstable, and disappointed in myself. I had to file for bankruptcy and work at the club six days a week into the wee hours of the morning to stay afloat. I popped Adderall and drank Red Bull to make it through the late nights. I felt exhausted, empty, and defeated. My life was a series of putting out fires, showing up to court dates, and trying my best to be an attentive mother. But my confidence took a major hit. While my soon-to-be ex-husband paraded his new woman around before our divorce was final, foreclosure notices stacked on my door, and the life I thought I had crumbled in front of my face.

I knew I needed to regain my confidence and I desperately wanted to feel good. I needed an anchor. Something to keep me from losing myself completely. I had the strong feeling that if I continued down the path I was on, sooner or later I would no longer recognize myself. I longed to return to the version of myself that was fun and spontaneous, but I felt like my pleasure had nowhere to fit between working late nights, taking care of my daughter, and everyday tasks. I thought it was quite selfish of me to desire pleasure when my life was in shambles. I had to work to get myself out of this mess. To do that would require effort and tenacity. When I was on the other side of this, I thought, then and only then would I consider doing things that made me feel good.

I started searching for inspirational quotes online, saying affirmations, and joining support groups, but none of it was working. One day I was standing in front of my mirror repeating some bullshit affirmation that I didn't believe and a small voice inside of me, clear as day, said, "Move. You can trust me." After 25+ years studying dance on a professional level, then working for several years as an exotic dancer and spending plenty of time "acting sexy," I realized that I had no movement practice of my own—something that wasn't performative or for the male gaze, but simply just for me. Guided by that small voice, I put my playlist on shuffle and moved my body for almost an hour straight. I twerked, twirled, rolled on the floor, cried, did African dance, stretched, jumped, and breathed deeply in silence.

That feeling of more that I craved, even before my world started to crumble, was right there. I had been overwhelmed by the drive to succeed on my own. I was buried beneath the pressure to increase my income, be a perfect mother, get out of crisis mode, and rebuild my life. Within that movement was everything I had been looking for. There was creativity, expression, flow, surrender, and attunement. *There was pleasure.*

I knew it would be a process to relearn how to trust my body and feel confident and powerful again, but I understood at that moment that I had just taken the first step.

This book is for driven women who are secretly suffering from a lack of pleasure in their lives. The pages that follow will show you how making one shift—the decision to begin moving your body with feminine intention—holds the key to reclaiming your most powerful self.

CHAPTER 1: The Driven Woman's Traits and Traumas

A driven woman is a go-getter who is intrinsically motivated to achieve. She often feels compelled to do so without much help from others. A driven, high achieving woman tends to be highly disciplined with structure and routines that she can count on to ensure she gets the outcome she desires. In other words, she makes shit happen. She can be counted on by the people in her life to come through when they need her, and there's never a lack of situations that can't seem to be fixed without her involvement. She is solution-based in her approach to life and prefers to take direct action as opposed to going with the flow.

The driven woman is busy and determined. She's not afraid to take risks, say the hard things, or make the tough decisions. The driven woman is not particularly interested in being soft or yielding because that's not how she's gotten where she is today. For some driven women, femininity is cute and novel—something to be saved for a spa weekend with the girls or to turn on for an anniversary dinner with a partner. She sees her femininity as something to put on *outside* of the workplace. Because she's not necessarily afraid of being alone, she can often take a my-way-or-the-highway approach in relationships. It's easy to hide her fear of being vulnerable behind hyper independence.

Trauma Responses

Often this hyper independence is a trauma response. **The important thing to know about trauma responses is that**

trauma isn't the thing that happened, but the effect left on our nervous system, soul, and psyche. This trauma can come from growing up in a household where you were forced to be a caregiver at a young age, from childhood bullying, having narcissistic parents, grief over a failed love affair, an abusive relationship, or losing a loved one.

Hyper independent women tend to be the rulers of the family and household. They run the show and take on all the responsibilities and decisions at home because they don't trust others to make the correct decision. This results in far too much responsibility on one person which can lead to overwhelm and an inability to cope with the pressure. When you are hyper independent you can become so used to doing everything yourself, making all the decisions, paying your own bills, and fixing all the issues that arise alone that asking for help becomes terrifying.

Even admitting that she's not coping is something a hyper independent woman will never dream of doing because that implies that she needs others to assist her, which is out of the question. This is exactly the state I was operating from as I navigated my divorce. I would rather die than have anyone think that I couldn't cope with the situation (even though I was stressed, exhausted, and barely hanging on by a thread).

Hyper independent women also tend to take on codependent relationships, as they feel their independence allows them to fix everything, including others. It feels safer having someone who needs them, rather than a person who will try to help them. It's not unusual for women with a hyper independent trauma response to treat their significant other as a service provider rather than a partner. This can lead to emasculating their partner and setting up an unhealthy dynamic in the relationship. Driven women often don't realize that the intensity that helped them get to where they are in life can be exhausting over time. Oftentimes, these women attract toxic partners because they are not afraid to put in work and will pick up the slack for a partner who doesn't give equal exchange. Putting in huge effort has gotten them to achieve some success in other areas of life, so why not apply that to relationships?

Ambition, in women, remains suspect because it breaks the expectation of servility. But, contrary to what society would have us think, being a driven woman isn't a negative thing. Driven women are passionate about bettering themselves and their lifestyle. There are many anecdotes about the uptight, rigid, domineering career woman who can't relax into the life she's created for herself, but we never hear about the upsides of being a go-getter. There is great accomplishment in being a person who can be relied upon. It's an incredibly powerful feeling to know that you can make things happen on your own, and self-reliance is an incredibly important skill. To be able to follow your own instincts and ideas should be applauded, especially in this time where, through social media and advertising, we are force-fed a collective mentality.

I'd also like to point out that being a driven woman does not always equal being a high income earner. There are women who may not have a high paying job, but they are incredibly hard working, relied upon by their families, actively in pursuit of a better lifestyle, and still make things happen (sometimes with little resources and no help). The ability to shoulder the weight and to be the person who moves the needle has become a badge of honor in this society.

The Pursuit of Pleasure

Whether a woman is experiencing great material success as a result of her ambition or working doggedly to change her circumstances, all this drive often leads to a lack of pleasure. And what is pleasure really? According to Oxford Languages, pleasure is "a feeling of happy satisfaction and enjoyment." Epicurean philosophy states that there are two types of pleasure: kinetic and katastematic.

Kinetic pleasure is derived from the act of doing (e.g. eating a delicious meal or having an intellectually stimulating conversation). Katastematic pleasure comes from *being* in a state. Think postcoital bliss or the feeling of being full from a delicious meal. Katastematic pleasure comes from a removal of unpleasant states and the absence of pain. We all experience pleasure differently as a result of differences in biology or neurochemistry but also as a result of past experiences.

From a brain chemistry perspective, there are four neurochemicals that are responsible for creating pleasure:

- Dopamine is the reward chemical, and we get it by satisfying an active goal like doing a self-care activity or completing a task.

- Oxytocin is the love hormone that's produced by hugging someone we love, playing with a pet, or having coffee with a friend.

- Endorphins are released as a response to pain or stress. Exercise, sex, and laughter all cause endorphins to be released in the body.

- Serotonin is the key hormone that stabilizes our moods. Sunlight, meditation, and time spent in nature all help boost serotonin.

Reflect & Release: Opt Out

As a driven woman myself, I have proudly worn the badge of busy for the last 10 years. It filled me with pride to know that I had things to do, appointments to keep, and people to meet. It fortified the fact that I was building something. I know now that the need to be busy all the time and the desire to be seen as a hard worker was a way of seeking validation. Who was I if I wasn't producing, moving the needle, and making things happen RIGHT NOW?!

These days, I am able to recognize my innate value as a human being and, when I start to feel overwhelmed and pressured to do all the things, this is what I do:

Pull out my mat.

Put on some meditation music.

Get on all fours (hands and knees).

Start to move my body incredibly slowly—slower than what even feels comfortable at the start.

Repeat silently or aloud, "Today, I opt out of urgency."

This practice takes no more than 5 minutes, but it sends the message to my body that, while I am still moving, I am calling my feminine energy back into balance. This practice reminds me that I can still DO but without the layers of urgency, stress, and forced energy. The next time you feel engulfed by your obligations, give it a try!

CHAPTER 2: The Consequences of Lacking Pleasure

The effects of a lack of pleasure in your life have a way of sneaking up on you because those effects often don't altogether feel like unhappiness. It's more like a slight gnawing, and you feel it growing over time. Every day you are confronted with your inability to shake the deep knowing that there is more to feel, do, and see than you are currently experiencing. There is a deep desire to get out of your head and into your body.

When you lack pleasure in your life, it's hard to be fully present. It can feel like you're on autopilot, just running around trying to have a perfect life, staying perpetually busy, and anticipating the needs of everyone else. There's nothing more painful than looking around and realizing you've become the sum total of the expectations of everyone around you. There's no harder pill to swallow than realizing that you've built a life, not based on what you truly desire, but on social conditioning, religious indoctrination, mommy culture, and capitalism.

When you are experiencing a lack of pleasure, it feels like something is missing. That can be jarring if you take a look around and, by all accounts, have what it takes to be deemed successful. You may have achieved the tangible goals of having a home, partner, children, career success, and material wealth. The thing is that having achieved those goals doesn't really have much to do with living a rich and fulfilling life as a fully expressed and empowered woman. Relationships, jobs, and material things can be taken from you at any moment. I had to learn that lesson the hard way, but you don't.

There is a direct correlation between pleasure and confidence. When you are tapped into what makes you feel good, nourished, and supported, you are less available for the things that make you feel devalued and disconnected. When you're experiencing joy and pleasure, you see the world and yourself in a more positive light, which also makes it easier to gain and maintain confidence in your abilities. When you're feeling good, you're much less likely to take every little critique and criticism to heart.

Lack of pleasure manifests in your body as rigidity, tightness, and the inability to flow. You may find that your sexual creativity or even your desire for sex is stifled. It manifests in your mind as guilt. When it's firmly planted in your mind that pleasure is something that you only give yourself permission to experience in dribs and drabs once you feel you've earned it, it leads to a feeling of guilt when you *gasp* experience it just because.

Fulfillment and Resentment

Let's go back and talk about the word "fulfilling." It's important that you understand that pleasure in and of itself doesn't necessarily lead to fulfillment. We can agree that laying oceanside every day, sipping champagne, and being fed chilled grapes by an insanely sexy person would no doubt be pleasurable, but, if that was how we spent every single day, would we feel fulfilled? Probably not. We want to create, we want to nurture, and we find value in working hard. It feels good to take care of the ones we love. Living a fulfilling life doesn't mean dropping all of these things, becoming a hedonist, and embarking on a wild goose chase for the next kinesthetically pleasurable thing.

To live a life of feminine fulfillment, pleasure needs to be integrated into your daily life. You are what you practice. It needs to be the foundation on which your life is built. A state of being that you cultivate daily. When you don't consciously cultivate joy and pleasure, you can easily miss the beauty, awe, and mystery that fills our world. Your world shrinks and becomes a series of tasks and obligations that you meet while feeling exhausted and burdened. You're greeting life with the feeling that if you can just check these things off, then and only then do you get to do something solely for enjoyment.

When you fail to cultivate pleasure in your own life, you'll leap without looking deep to the first person who offers it to you. It's easy to run full speed into the arms of the first person who makes you "feel good" if you haven't spent any time considering what makes you feel good and actually integrating it into your life. If you are already partnered and have a family, a lack of pleasure will lead you right down the path to becoming an overwhelmed mom and resentful wife. When you are the scheduler, cook, cleaning woman, car service, organizer, and overall household manager, without pleasure in your life, that resentment rises to the surface faster than a bubble in a champagne glass. Trust me, no one feels less like having sex than a woman seething under a cloak of resentment.

A lack of pleasure can affect your sex life, which, in turn, affects the relationship. Also, if you're not experiencing your own joy, how excited are you going to be when your partner invites you to do something that they find pleasurable that doesn't exactly light you up? You'll suck it up and watch the *Paw Patrol* movie for the fourteenth time with your kid because that's what moms do, right? But if your partner wants to check out a band they're into that you don't really love, you're not available for that. When you don't take time for the things that fill your own cup, you're much less likely to indulge your significant other in their fancies and, over time, that can create problems in the relationship.

If you have a career that is demanding and takes up a lot of your life, despite the fact that you're well-compensated, without joy and pleasure as the foundation of your life, you can easily fall down a rabbit hole of comfortable misery. You're able to have the material things you desire, but it feels like you're wearing golden handcuffs. It may be that you're even throwing yourself into your work just because it feels better to be constantly moving and producing than sitting with the fact that you are unfulfilled. This feeling of unfulfillment manifests in the body as stress, numbness, and an overall tension and rigidity. It shows up as headaches, jaw tension, and joint stiffness. You're also at risk for falling into self-destructive behavior patterns like overeating, drinking to excess, risky sexual behavior, and disappearing into online games and social media.

Leading a pleasure-filled life is not about shirking responsibilities and living a completely self-absorbed existence. It's about balance. It's about awareness and the management of your energy. It is the defiant rejection of a patriarchal capitalist society designed to suck the life out of us. It is the refusal to accept a life spent on auto-pilot. It's a blueprint for calling back home the pieces of yourself you've lost along the way.

Reflect & Release: Recalling Pleasure

In the midst of my divorce process, when life was a series of tasks that drained the life out of me, and there was nothing but bad news at every turn, it was hard for me to conjure up feelings of joy or pleasure. I had to look to the past to remember the version of myself that was playful, amorous, and lighthearted.

When you're feeling tight, stressed, and disconnected from pleasure, try this:

Find a photo of yourself taken in a moment where you were truly joyful.

Breathe deeply and take it all in—your facial expression, the background scenery, any other beloved people in the photo with you.

Allow the corners of your mouth to turn up as you let your body relax into remembering.

Turn on music you love (could be associated with that time in your life, or not).

Move.

Holding the image of your joyful self in your mind with music playing, just move in whatever way you feel called to. The first time I did this, I burst into tears. It was a sweet release because I realized the joyful spirit inside of me wasn't gone forever. I just had to be more intentional about bringing it forward.

CHAPTER 3: Making Space for Co-Existing Truths

According to Dr. Brené Brown, a research professor who specializes in shame, vulnerability, and leadership, women most often experience shame as a web of layered, conflicting, and competing expectations. These expectations tell us who we should be, what we should be, and how we should be. At their core, these ideals are products of very rigid social and community expectations. They present very narrow interpretations of who women are "supposed to be" based on demographics (e.g., their gender, race, class, sexual orientation, age, religious identity) and/or our roles (e.g., a mother, employee, partner, group member).

Societal Expectations and Shame

When we don't measure up to these expectations, the result is often shame. Shame, however, makes us feel trapped, powerless, and isolated. So many of us want to see versions of ourselves that are soft and feminine, yet strong and powerful, but we find ourselves defeated by a superficial society. We become who we think we need to be in order to be loved, accepted, and successful. In doing so, we give away our power. In a world of curated Instagram feeds, families doing cute Tik Tok challenges together, and mommy blogs that seem to exist solely for the purpose of making us feel like shit, no one wants to admit to being at odds with the expectations that are placed on us.

There is a certain audacity it takes to admit that, despite having all the trappings of a "successful life," we may not be entirely fulfilled. In this culture of oversharing, there is an enormous pressure to prove to friends, family, and strangers on the internet alike that we are content. It takes courage to admit that, underneath our vacation photos, happy hours, and shiny new purchases, we are experiencing anxiety, sexlessness, and fatigue.

Toxic Positivity

Wellness culture often perpetuates ideas of toxic positivity and permanent optimism, leaving us feeling guilty for admitting, even if only to ourselves, that we aren't able to "rise above" any negative emotion we are feeling. According to toxic positivity, gratitude is the solution to everything. Feeling down? You must not be practicing gratitude. Want to attract better experiences into your life? Write down 10 things you are grateful for. Want to have a productive day? Start with an attitude of gratitude. Seriously, it's like give me a damn break already! The problem with gratitude is that it can invalidate our experiences and trigger shame. We are human beings who can hold contradictory feelings. We can feel grateful for what we have in our lives and also want more.

Moreover, gratitude shouldn't be practiced in a way that compares ourselves to others. It's not about who has it worse or better. I can't tell you how many times I dismissed my own unhappiness because I felt it couldn't compete with something someone else had gone through. You have to understand that your experience can exist at the same time with others who have it worse and be equally worthy of receiving help. The thing about the Suffering Olympics is no one ever really wins.

Sadly, many women lack a trusted circle of friends that they can confide in, a circle who can hold space for them to express when they are not okay. There is very little mentorship when it comes to living a pleasure-filled life because it's seen as a radical way to live. We are taught from a very young age to be people pleasers, never how to feel 100% comfortable on the receiving end of pleasure. We aren't taught how to integrate it into our lives. Instead, we are indoctrinated to see pleasure as something way over there. Something we can only attain after we've fulfilled our duties, achieved a certain goal, or have been designated as deserving. If we're looking to make more money, lose weight, find a partner, or fix our credit, there are a plethora of people out there ready to coach us into success. When it comes to leading a balanced life of fulfillment, however, there are not nearly as many options.

Reflect & Release: Moving Through Emotions

I'm a pretty even-keeled person who doesn't often find herself in the throes of anger. When I do, it can be very jarring. I used to feel like it was not a welcome feeling, so my response was to try to bottle it up, push it down, and hope it would dissipate. I understand now that darker emotions have just as much right to be expressed as positive ones. In fact, it's essential that they are.

When I feel emotions like anger, jealousy, fear or sadness, rather than put up resistance, I move with them. The next time you are feeling any of these emotions, resist the urge to continue on with a tight smile and a reply of "I'm fine" to anyone who asks. Instead:

Put on some metal or emo music or whatever you feel. If you're feeling grief, put on some gospel music and rock and sway.

Move as anger or jealousy. Give those feelings a physical form.

Thrash about, have a solo pillow fight, find something of little consequence and break it.

Maybe you'll cry. Giving a physical expression to negative emotions dramatically lessens the chances of being consumed by them.

CHAPTER 4: The Remedies and Elements of Movement

Movement creates a bridge between mind, body and spirit. When you get lost in movement, the veil between the physical and spiritual dimension thins, creating the perfect portal to access the deeper parts of you. You can tap into your body's self-healing powers, unleash your creativity, and develop greater emotional intelligence. To mindfully move your body is to have a conversation with your higher self.

In this age of technology, we are constantly stimulated and, to make matters worse, most people are movement deficient. We are thinking and processing more and moving less, and it's causing stress, blockages, and feelings of disharmony. Every day we lose ourselves in other people's lives—whether on social media or in news stories full of fear and despair. Tuning into ourselves takes a conscious effort. Moving the body offers us an antidote to overwhelm and a way through emotional obstruction.

Movement is the Remedy

Movement affects everything, from circulation to digestion to metabolism to immunity. It also plays a significant role in improving mental health. It keeps your mind sharp as you age and reduces the risk of depression and anxiety. It also improves creativity by giving your brain a much needed "cognitive pause," helping you change your perception and come up with new ideas.

Because our society places the highest value on productivity and progress, our bodies take the role of subordinate, working beneath our mind. We seldom listen to our bodies until they are literally screaming to us in the form of headaches, chronic pain, and illness. Diet culture equates movement with exercise. However, movement is more than just exercise and does not necessarily require effort, though it does require action.

For women, studies have shown that regularly moving the body may increase sexual function and arousal. Consistent movement enhances sexual satisfaction indirectly by preserving autonomic flexibility, which benefits cardiovascular health and mood. Positive body image due to consistent movement practices also increases sexual well-being. Moving with Feminine Intention is a certain way of moving that requires that you work with these three elements: exploration, flow, and sensation.

Exploration

Most movements we do are not done in the spirit of exploration; the goal of the movement is execution. Whether it's a jog, a Zumba class, or weightlifting session, there is an end goal. You aim to run for a certain amount of time, get the sequence of the movement down, or complete a certain number of reps. There is a specific goal in mind, and your job is to get it done. Taking action is a quality associated with masculine energy. When you are not moving in a specific way with an intended result and are simply moving to notice, observe, and become aware, you are Moving with Feminine Intention. Movement exploration is about wholeness instead of perfection. There is never a right or wrong way to do any movement. You are simply being receptive to new awareness of your body and how it moves through space.

Flow

To move with feminine intention also requires the element of flow. By definition, flow means a steady and continuous stream. Feminine movement isn't a series of predetermined steps or shapes. It's letting layer after layer unfold, one movement leading to the next. It's a continuous action without stopping to think of how it looks, if it's correct, or if it makes sense. Feminine energy is free-flowing and not bound by rules; it is not restrictive and does not abide by social norms. You should approach movement the same way. Let me be clear: Incorporating the element of flow doesn't mean that your movements must be soft, delicate, or graceful; it simply means that you are allowing the layers to unfold and the movement to build on itself.

Sensation

Sensation is the last element that must be present when Moving with Feminine Intention. This is how we experience pleasure. MovFi, or Moving with Feminine Intention, is activating the senses to create full body awareness. What parts of our body do we instinctively touch when we move? Where do our eyes tend to land? Do we move to the music or a rhythm inside our own mind? Do we move differently based on the aroma in the room? What particular movements stir something inside? These are all questions that are answered by this practice.

What you'll find is that moving in this way regularly will start to change the way you experience the world around you. You'll start to attune more deeply to whatever environment you're in. Your everyday pedestrian movements may become a bit smoother or have more flair. You will find yourself being more *present*. The ability to fully give your attention to the moment rather than dwelling on the past or trying to predict future events plays such an integral role in our overall health and well-being. And, contrary to popular belief, sitting still for 30 minutes while chanting *ohm* is not the only way to find it!

Reflect & Release: Do What Feels Good

My movement practice has evolved so much from the first day I heard the call to move intuitively. Having spent so much of my life immersed in dance training, my natural tendency, even when dancing alone, was to default to movements that I already knew I looked good doing. It took a while for me to release the idea that moving my body was solely a performative act and truly become curious. It is such a liberating feeling to give into your body's urge to do a certain movement, regardless of who you are or who is around.

Try this: Next time you're in the grocery store and you see they've restocked your favorite snack item and you kind of wanna jump for joy, do it!

Out at the park and the warm breeze on your skin makes you want to twirl? Go for it!

Vacuuming the living room and get the urge to twerk? Have at it!

Become curious about how your body wants to move, regardless of how that movement looks.

CHAPTER 5: Re(Introduction) to Moving with Feminine Intention

When you've spent most of your life locked in your head—thinking, ruminating, and worrying, only attending to your body if it demands your attention or you want it to do something for you—the concept of Moving with Feminine Intention daily can seem challenging. Overstimulating the mind is the new addiction, but a balanced life requires you to transcend the limitations of your mind by getting into your body.

If you've been looking outside of your own body to feel at home, it's likely led to distrust in your decision-making, lack of confidence in yourself as a sensual being, and an inability to regulate your nervous system. When you are at home in your body, you are connected to the intelligence outside of your brain. You are in tune with sensation, intuition, and instinct. Being in tune leads to confident decision-making, the ability to be present, and an abundance of sensual pleasure.

Dysregulation and Self-Regulation

The nervous system is the major controlling, regulatory, and communicating system in the body. It is the center of all mental activity, including thought, learning, and memory. Together, with the endocrine system, the nervous system is responsible for regulating and maintaining homeostasis. Through its receptors, the nervous system keeps us in touch with our external and internal environments. A regulated nervous system allows you to harmonize with the energies at play in any given situation. Dysregulation will cause a person to non-consciously and physically hold onto the stress charge in the muscle and fascia tissue (connective tissue that surrounds and holds everything in the body in place). This creates a struggle to manage emotions, leaving you feeling ungrounded and susceptible to viewing your life through the lens of anxiety, stress, and chronic fatigue.

Moving with Feminine Intention is a wonderful tool for self-regulation. It allows you to follow what you feel with motion and ultimately discharge emotions that are meant to flow. It's such a satisfying release to let go of unwanted feelings and unprocessed emotions. MovFi also allows you to call *in* states of being that you want to experience. You can practice affirmation through movement and build muscle memory around feelings of joy, ease, and sexual confidence. The body is a map of every experience you've ever had and a masterful keeper of your emotional history. The mind wants to give you the life that makes sense on paper. You have to consult your whole being if you want a life that brings you the kind of satisfaction you can feel deep down in your bones. Your heart. Your gut. Your body. When you move your body with feminine intention daily, you can measure what's happening in your life relative to your practice.

Connecting through MovFi

When you are tapped into feminine intention, you trust in your decision-making and move from a place of power and authority in your life. You'll bend, but you won't break. You may crack, but you won't shatter. You are firmly rooted in who you are and simply won't allow yourself to be at the whim of others' demands, expectations, and judgements. Circumstances won't dictate how you approach life. The gag is, the more rooted you are, the more flexible you become. MovFi brings you back into connection with the wisdom in your body. Your instincts become sharper, intuition becomes stronger, and you develop ultimate trust in your decisions.

MovFi connects you to your sensual self. By simply knowing what feels good to your body, you are able to experience sexual pleasure on a whole new level. You can create your own state of arousal before a partner ever enters the picture, *if* a partner ever enters the picture. Of course your sensual self is more than just who you are as a sexual being. Your sensuality lies in the awareness, the slowness, the taking in of all things delightful. It's noticing how, when you crack the crust of crème brulée with your spoon, it feels like you're breaking ground on your dream home. It's being able to relax into touch as if you're being wrapped into your favorite blanket. It's allowing yourself to be transported by a smell. It's being able to be present enough to notice beauty around you.

Discovering through MovFi

We've been conditioned to think of the body as something to push, mold, and shape to our liking. MovFi invites you to view the body as something to be listened to. Your body speaks the language of movement. If you want to know the deepest secrets of your soul, DANCE. Many women simply aren't aware of what a powerful tool MovFi is. To some, it feels too "woo woo," and the results aren't tangible enough. It's understood that if you make running a practice, after some time you'll likely lose a little weight. If you practice yoga every day, eventually you'll become more flexible. But with MovFi, you don't actually know what you will uncover and that can be scary. It's a journey of self-discovery that can feel intimidating to engage in alone. It's a big deal to move your body in new and different ways when you've spent most of your life moving in the same linear way. It's an even bigger deal when you have internalized shame around sensual movement, self-touch, and erotic expression.

One of the most important things MovFi does is allow you to find a sense of safety in your own body, which can digest the things that the brain couldn't deal with at the time and stored away. This is why MovFi is so helpful in releasing trauma. Remember, trauma isn't the thing that happened to us, but the effect left on our nervous system and psyche. Through movement, you increase your ability to self-soothe by connecting with the flow of pleasurable sensation moving through the body.

MovFi focuses on learning how to sense your body, and is less concerned with how you position your body. Women will say to me, "Hey, I go to a pole dance class and I take heels dance classes. Isn't that the same thing?" It's not. You are learning to position your body and move in ways that are designed to appear sensual or sexy. Of course, once you master these modalities, you can start to infuse the elements of exploration, flow, and sensation, but, at the onset, you are learning how to do certain movements that society deems sexy.

It's very rare in a recreational dance class to be instructed to pay attention to your breath, to how certain movements feel, or to get an explanation as to why you are doing a particular movement. I was a master at executing movements that were designed to entice from a slight tilt of my head to a big body roll, but there was absolutely no present-time awareness of my body taking place. With proper guidance in a safe container, women can learn to develop their own practice and feel confident in their ability to feel pleasure in their bodies, shift their energy, release emotions, and feel grounded (or whatever experience is needed on that particular day).

Reflect & Release: Self-Regulate

Connecting to the breath is one of the most simple ways to self-regulate. At the time, I didn't have the language for it or recognize it as a practice. I was just trying to keep my shit together. Whenever I would pull up to the courthouse during my divorce proceedings, I would park my car, sit up very straight in my seat, and take three very deep breaths. I didn't close my eyes. I was aware of the motion around me, but those breaths allowed me to find some inner balance before walking into a tense combative and high stress situation.

The next time you find yourself in an anxious state or stressful situation, try it:

Sit up straight.

Inhale deeply through your nose with your mouth closed.

Exhale through your mouth with your lips pursed as if you were whistling or kissing.

Repeat as many times as you need to.

CHAPTER 6: Committing to Your Whole Self

Power can't be obtained from outside forces. Attention, validation, and acknowledgement are all nice things, but, by Moving with Feminine Intention, you are cultivating power that comes from within. This type of power isn't concerned with validation or attention. This power is like an infinite fire that keeps you glowing from the inside out. It doesn't need anyone to keep feeding it more wood, nor can it be extinguished by someone dousing it with water (or destructive criticism). Our body is our greatest ally in living a full, vibrant, fully expressed life. Moving with Feminine Intention connects us with our body in the most intimate way possible, allowing body, mind, and spirit to work together to create a strong internal guidance system and lead us to a life that feels expansive.

You Are Your Best Resource

The truth is: You have the answers. And you've always had them. They are not in your girlfriends' advice, your tarot cards, your Google search, your self-help book, or your guru. They are within you. The work is in creating practices that affirm this knowing and becoming able to access it and use it to create change in your life. So what does that look like? My longtime client Melissa M. describes it this way: "Just taking the time, even if it's just a few minutes, to be feminine inside movement is incredibly therapeutic and healing. When I first started, I was kind of mechanical and tried to move exactly how Lily was moving. Through experience, I've learned what feels good in my own body. Over time, the principles of MovFi took root in my own being and I have so much more comfort in my daily walk."

MovFi is one practice out of many that I help my clients cultivate when they are suffering from a lack of pleasure, but it's absolutely the most important one because, through movement, you are able to circumvent the anxiety-ridden thought loops that come up when you attempt to make a change in your life. The ones that say, "Who do you think you are? This life isn't good enough for you? You've never been confident, what makes you think you can start now? You? Powerful? Ha! You're just not feminine enough. That won't ever change."

Out of Our Heads and Into Our Bodies (Consistently)

I love what Philip Shepard, author of *Radical Wholeness*, says about the life we are choosing when we resign ourselves to living in our heads:

> "All of our tendencies towards disconnection are merely extensions of our relationship with our bodies. But there is a deeper reason that our disconnection from the body is so injurious to all: When you disconnect from your body, you are disconnecting from the richest and most tangible reality of your being. To do that habitually—to cut yourself off from the reality of your being as a reflex—is to eventually alienate yourself from being.

> When you are alienated from being, you can never feel truly secure, because the foundation of true security is a security of being—an experience of your reality in all its fullness. It's

what you discover when you come home to the body, and feel the self as a whole, and come to rest within that whole in the timelessness of the present and the world to which it belongs. There is simply no substitute—not even in all the amassed conquests and acquisitions on which the tyrant fixates. If you are not grounded in that security of being, an undercurrent of anxiety will run through all that you undertake, gnawing at you even when you just sit still. That is the condition to which we consign ourselves by living in the head."

MovFi invites you to make a commitment to your whole self by creating a practice and showing up for that practice on a consistent basis. Most of us have plenty of experience with showing up to something only when you feel like it, when all the circumstances are perfect, and we're in the right headspace. Keep in mind that, through MovFi, you are opening yourself up to pleasure and forming a relationship with your body. You must simply be available. You can practice here and there, and you'll feel really good…now and then. Like any valued relationship, being available for it, even when it's not convenient, is paramount.

When you practice daily, you can measure what's happening in your life relative to your practice. Over time, that starts to lessen the urgency of feelings of anxiety, overwhelm, and hesitancy. The question I often get from clients is how long? "How long do I practice moving in this way before I start to feel like this confident, attuned, present woman?" I'm sorry to bust your bubble, but this isn't a formulaic one-size-fits-all practice. What takes root for you in two weeks might take someone else two months. Don't forget the first element of Moving with Feminine Intention is exploration! It's not a rush to the finish line.

Reflect and Release: Write Your Soul Vows

We make all kinds of vows and oaths professionally (and to partners) but rarely to ourselves. We take our commitments to others very seriously, but rarely do we intentionally commit to ourselves.

There is power in making a public declaration about how you promise to treat yourself. Put your most cherished vision for your life and how you choose to honor yourself on paper.

Writing things down helps clarify your intentions, keeps you engaged, and helps you process and recognize your emotions. It's a wonderful complement to movement.

Soul vows serve as an intention, expression, and commitment to self-love.

I keep my soul vows where I can see them and read them every morning as part of my practice. Moving with Feminine Intention every day is something I have committed to. Even if it's just for one song, it's built my confidence to know that I am a person who honors commitments to myself.

Conclusion

When that aha moment onstage in the club prompted me to start moving my body with feminine intention as a practice for myself, it brought up a lot of inner discord. On the one hand, it felt like I was getting to know myself again, and that was beautiful and satisfying. But, on the other hand, this newfound inner knowing highlighted the ways in which I was not living in alignment with the truth of who I was. It became clear that working as a stripper was no longer serving me. I knew that a change of location was necessary, and I understood that I had to forgive myself for ignoring the red flags in my marriage. If I didn't, there was a life full of bitterness and unwillingness to trust again that was ready to welcome me.

Of course, I couldn't change all of these things right away, but I had *direction*. Without direction, you feel stuck. When you use MovFi to develop a deep connection to your body, it is easier to sense when you are out of accord with the truth. Once I acknowledged this disconnect within myself, I was able to do the necessary work to realign. I could set about doing the work that was required to make the changes. I could hold this vision of the life I wanted in my mind and express it with my body. I could connect to the actual feeling I wanted this new version of myself to have daily, if just for a few minutes. And *that* was the source of power and energy I used to do the practical things required to build the life I wanted to be living.

Even as a trained dancer since the age of 4 years old then later making a career out of moving my body, it wasn't until I started doing this work that I was able to access the inner confidence necessary to make big changes in my life. I knew how to *perform* confidence very well, and was good at taking risks when I knew I had a soft place to land. The ability to move forward with an un-wavering belief in myself and to seek out pleasure along the way is a direct result of making a daily practice out of moving my body in this way.

One of the best pieces of feedback I've received from a client about MovFi is "It put a process and a practice into what I always hear and never know how to do." I love that because I know that there are so many women who hear these platitudes (love your body, be mindful, trust your intuition), but no one ever shows us *how* to embody a mindful woman who loves her body and trusts her intuition. We're only taught to understand intellectually that this is what we *should* be doing.

Women have sacrificed their relationship with their bodies for long enough and, in doing so, have relinquished access to the personal power that comes with being connected to their embodied wisdom. It's time to reclaim that power. Here are two ways that I can assist you:

Join our Facebook community

Pleasure Principles for Driven Women with Lily Shepard. If you found value in this book, then you'll deepen your relationship to pleasure even more in the group. It's designed with the specific intention of helping you reclaim power in your life through intuitive movement. I share ways to shape your capacity to care for yourself and reorient your life to one that goes beyond just being blessed to be alive. The goal is to create a life that's nourishing and even exciting. On top of that, you'll connect with other amazing women who are committed the same journey. It's private, so only members can see who's in the group and what's posted. And it's FREE (for now, at least)!

Book a call with me

Let's talk. Me and you. About how you want to feel compared to how you actually feel, and how to cross over. I create spaces, for individuals, small and large groups, to learn how to listen to and trust their bodies.

Scan me or visit www.lilyshepardmoves.com to get started.

About Me

I've been training in dance since I was four years old. I have a bachelor's degree in dance, studied abroad in Jamaica, and performed on big stages in Las Vegas for 11 years, including at a Billboard Awards show with Beyonce. I also spent a large part of that time as an exotic dancer. I love the freedom of dance—embracing your own style, releasing stress, and gaining strength. I didn't realize, however, until I hit a rock bottom that there was science behind the stress relief and a spiritual component to movement. I went from pretending to be confident in my body and happy with my life to actually loving all of it. Intuitive movement has not only opened this door for me but for hundreds of women who I've guided back into their bodies.

As a Pleasure Coach and Embodiment Specialist, I create space for women to move their bodies without judgment while offering opportunities for them to address their traumas and struggles while reclaiming their power. I apply decades of dance training; 200 hours of certified trauma-informed yoga instruction; and my personal experience to my work with high achieving professional women. I'm passionate about the power of movement and how to use it in such a way that it births the inner confidence and trust that's necessary to design a life that not only looks good, but feels good deep down in your spirit.

If my work excites your spirit, or even sparks a little curiosity, head over to Lilyshepardmoves.com to learn more about my offerings and see how we can work together.

Lightning Source UK Ltd.
Milton Keynes UK
UKHW022339261022
411154UK00011B/170

9 798986 003900